To John,
my husband and best friend,
thank you for:

- the way you make me feel like someone very special every day;
- the way your patience, kindness, and confidence in me always show up at the right time; and
- the way you encourage my dreams and then do your best to make them all come true.

Contents

Foreword   vii
Acknowledgements   xiii

1. General Behaviour   1
2. Table Manners   11
3. Setting the Table   16
4. Finger Foods   25
5. Telephone Etiquette   30
6. Common Courtesies   37
7. Etiquette in the Workplace   41

Manners and Etiquette: An Epilogue   47

Foreword

"What is another word for etiquette?" This is the first question I ask the students as I start my seminars in Vancouver, B.C. Most students, because they know why they have come to the seminar, know that *etiquette* is another word for GOOD MANNERS.

One of the students came back with a question for me. "Where did etiquette start?" I was delighted to hear this question from a child, and I immediately started researching it. Before I commence my book on etiquette and manners, I would like to share with you a brief summary of the origin of etiquette and good manners. I believe that you will find this short history of manners as interesting as I did.

The word *etiquette* is derived from an old French word, *estiquer,* and that in turn from an old German word, *stechen,* both of which are verbs meaning "to stick" or "to affix." Some etymologists conjecture that centuries ago, regulations to be observed at court (or, possibly, in a barracks) were posted or stuck to a support or wall and eventually became *l'estiquet* or *l'estiquette* (the rules for the day), hence *etiquette.* In France today, the code of polite social conduct is generally termed *règles du savoir vivre* ("rules of knowing how to live"). In English-speaking countries, such rules, whether they are guides for ceremonies or deal with ordinary social conventions, such as setting a table, are generally classified as *etiquette.*

In England, the first book to call its contents rules of etiquette was *The Fine Gentleman's Etiquette or, Lord Ches-*

terfield's Advice to His Son, verified 1776. However, books on etiquette did not really flourish until the nineteenth century, with the advance of the Industrial Revolution. The old distinctions between "superiors" and "inferiors" was once accepted unquestioningly and were so well understood that only occasionally did "rules" need to be repeated as required safeguards. The early purpose of etiquette, once it moved outside royal and aristocratic circles and began to be applied to ordinary social life, appears to have been the hallmark of the upper class. *Etiquette; or, A Guide to the Usages of Society* (1830) makes this opening statement: "Etiquette is the barrier which society draws around itself as a protection . . . a shield against the intrusion of the impertinent, the improper, and the vulgar—a guard against those obtuse persons who, having neither talent or delicacy, would be continually thrusting themselves into a society to whom their presence might . . . be offensive and even insupportable."

Etiquette books explained the rituals and rules followed by nineteenth-century upper-class society. Thus newcomers to wealth were aided in concealing their social inexperience and were more readily accepted by those of accepted social station.

American proponents of etiquette before the Civil War rejected English and Continental formalities as undemocratic, but by the 1880s many Americans reversed their attitudes and welcomed formalities. Special manuals described ballroom etiquette, and anyone setting out for New York—the acknowledged fount of American etiquette at that time—would do well to secure a copy of *Social Etiquette of New York.*

In other parts of the world, cultural or religious customs keep a stronger hold on etiquette, and sometimes this is markedly different from situations where one might expect to find similarities. For example, in the Middle East cultural customs still dominate Bedouin dining etiquette. The hand (preferably the right hand) is used in eating, and the communal pot is dipped into by hand. However, urban Arab society now follows the rules of Western behaviour and uses standard cutlery and serving procedures. At Japanese tables it is bad form to top rice with other food, while Chinese people heap their food on a bed of rice.

As far as we know, principles of polite behaviour were first set down in an ancient Egyptian manuscript, *The Instructions of Ptah Hotep,* around 2500 B.C. Conduct is also discussed in several sections of the Bible, but the earliest explicit rules of propriety appeared in a special section of the Talmud. The earliest work known from a European source is *The Treatise on Courtesy,* written about A.D. 1200.

Numerous etiquette manuals were published on both sides of the Atlantic, beginning about 1830. Most of them monotonously parroted each other's phrases. No authoritative work on this topic appeared anywhere until 1922. At this date, an American, Emily Post, wrote *Etiquette, the Blue Book of Social Usage.* It covered almost every possible social contingency in detail as never before. After that, books on etiquette were written fast and furiously. In the 1960s and 1970s, etiquette once again declined; manners and respect appear to have been ignored due to the ascendency of an almost overwhelming "popular culture"—a culture that possibly did not condone vulgarity but most certainly tolerated it.

Now we are in the nineties, and I would like to see good manners and respect for each other once again back in our daily routine—back to basics, starting with Please, Thank you, May I?, and Excuse me.

The following pages will provide practical information on social etiquette as currently practised in North America and Great Britain and the many other countries that have been influenced by British civilization. I assure the readers that the following information on etiquette is definitely current.

Mary Kennedy welcoming her students to her Seminar on Manners and Etiquette at the Hotel Vancouver in Vancouver, British Columbia.

Acknowledgements

To Ian,

- who has always impressed me with his knowledge of the literary word,
- who has been a fount of knowledge during the times he "critiqued" my book, and
- whom I thank from the bottom of my heart for all his help and encouragement.

To Tricia,

- who supported my idea from the day I started my own business and encouraged me to make it come to fruition,
- for being my friend.

MARY KENNEDY'S
WORLD OF SOCIAL
ETIQUETTE

1

General Behaviour

I ask my students at the seminar to make a list of what they think are good manners and bad manners.

1. "Please" / "thank you"
2. "Excuse me"
3. Addressing people correctly
4. Not interrupting
5. Eye contact while talking to people
6. Thank-you cards
7. Giving seat up (public transportation)
8. Listening to what people are saying
9. Standing up
10. Taking hats off when entering a building, e.g., home or restaurant
11. Opening doors for other people

1. No please or thank you
2. Elbows on table
3. Snatching
4. Talking in class
5. Vulgarity
6. Tardiness (being late)
7. Speaking in a language other people cannot understand
8. Leaving hats on while any national anthem is being played at sports events

I think the above list is excellent. The students don't name everything on the list each time, but over the course of the past five years this list has grown, and I keep adding to it.

Why don't I talk a little about each item on the list.

"Please" / "Thank you." This is getting down to basics. Every child should be taught to say "please" and "thank you" from the moment they learn to speak. It is hard at first to get toddlers to say these two very important phrases, but if parents persist, it really pays off.

"Excuse me." Use when:

· You don't hear something that was said to you;
· if you accidentally bump into someone or walk in front of someone; and
· if you wish to leave the room or someone's company.

These two little expressions sound so absolutely correct when they are used in the right context.

Addressing people correctly. I really do feel very uncomfortable when a young child addresses me by my first name. Unless told to do otherwise, children should always address older people by their title, Mr., Mrs., Miss, or Ms. In England, our close friends' children often call us Auntie or Uncle, which doesn't sound quite so formal. I enjoy being "Auntie" to so many more children than my nieces and nephews.

Not interrupting. There is nothing worse than trying to have a conversation with another adult when children insist on interrupting. They should be encouraged to stand and wait patiently until the adult turns and asks them what they want or asks them to participate in the conversation. We realize that now is the important moment to a child, but they have to be taught to wait; and patience is a virtue that they will use in many other social situations. We also recognize that children should be encouraged to converse with adults, but at appropriate times.

Eye contact while talking to people. I always feel that if people don't look at you while they are talking, they are not comfortable about what they are saying or they may not be telling the truth. It is such a confidence builder to be able to look people straight in the eye and tell them how or what you feel in a simple and straightforward manner. Also, this well-known technique encourages honesty and confidence for both parties.

Thank-you cards. If someone has taken the trouble to buy, wrap, and give you a gift, return the compliment by recognizing his/her gesture of friendship or appreciation. Telephone or write a card to let the gift giver know you are thinking of him/her. If you take the trouble to thank a person for a present or anything else, you are reinforcing his/her perception that you are a very special person.

Giving up seat (public transportation). I'm afraid this is sadly lacking today. I sometimes travel by our Skytrain into Vancouver, and if an eldery, pregnant, or handicapped person gets on the train, I will gladly give up my seat if the train is full. If there are children sitting, I wait for a few minutes to see if they will give up their seat. It appears that very few of today's children have been instructed in this common courtesy to mature adults.

One of the students in my program stated that he would gladly vacate his seat for a person in more need than himself but felt reluctant to do so because of peer pressure—the fear of being laughed at by friends. This is where confidence comes in; if children have been taught good manners, they will have the confidence to act accordingly and not worry about what their peers think, because they know they are doing the correct thing.

Listening to what people are saying. Listening is a wonderful skill! But not many people can do it for any length of time. This is something people have to teach themselves to do. A good and attentive listener will go far, for a good listener learns much from those listened to and gains the confidence and trust of the speaker.

Standing up. It certainly does impress a lady when a gentleman stands up as she enters the room. This is a common courtesy, and not a difficult courtesy, but not too many men observe this protocol. When a man *does* stand up when a lady enters the room he receives silent commendation from all present.

Taking hats off when entering a building, e.g., home or restaurant. This is one of my pet peeves. Even in the nineties, I think it is very bad manners for gentlemen, young or old, to sit in a restaurant, or even a public office like a bank, with their baseball caps or hats still perched on their heads. This courtesy applies especially when entering a home—hats should come off. It is common courtesy and simple good manners. If a father does not remove his hat, certainly his son won't know that he should. Once when I asked a young man in church to remove his baseball cap, he looked at me in amazement; he honestly did not know that he was being bad-mannered or irreverent. He just didn't know any better.

I must add that some religions do allow gentlemen to wear certain headgear at all times—for example, Sikh gentlemen wear their turbans wherever they go, including when they are in uniform, and Jewish gentlemen wear the *kippah* (skullcaps) when they go to the synagogue and in the home. We must respect other people's cultures and religions, especially in Vancouver, where we are a multicultural community and should be proud of the fact.

Opening Doors for Other People. At all of our seminars I ask my students if they think this is old-fashioned, and I am always amazed when the students say no. As I go into a shopping mall, I always look behind as I walk through the entrance, and if there is someone coming I will keep the door open for him. It is very rude to let a door slam as someone else is trying to enter, and ruder yet if a person following you is carrying something. When students are dressed up for their graduation ceremonies and dinner/dance, it really makes a young lady feel very special when her date opens the car door for her when she gets in and out of the car. This courtesy should be followed up by holding the door open when they go into any building. There is nothing old-fashioned about that, just simple basic respect and good manners. Also, older people particularly appreciate this courtesy.

Elbows on the table. If your elbows are on the table, then you are also slouching and taking up the space of the person sitting next to you. Elbows on the table are basically an indication of an improper upbringing or a less than casual attitude towards good manners.

Snatching. I ask my students what snatching can lead to and always get the same reply: "Anger, fighting, bad feelings." It is so much better to ask, "May I please?" and request the item be passed to you in a proper manner.

Talking in class. Very bad manners—lack of respect to your teacher, to those students around you, and most of all to yourself.

Vulgarity. Profanity is very prevalent these days, especially since people hear so much of it in the popular media of movies and television. If one gets into the habit of swearing, it is a hard habit to break. I am dismayed when I hear young people swearing. Some think it is the macho thing to do, but the bottom line is that swearing is *never* appropriate.

Tardiness (being late). I always tend to be a little on the early side. I get very upset if I am running late for an appointment. It is extremely bad-mannered for people to arrive late, especially at a dinner party when the host and hostess have asked you for a specific time. Even at the theatre, when most people are in their seats, there always seems to be one person climbing over everyone just as the performance is about to start.

Speaking in a language other people cannot understand. We have many different languages spoken in Vancouver; this creates a pleasant ambiance in our city and helps to make it an interesting place to live. But when there is a group of people talking together, it is definitely incorrect to start talking in a language that is not understood by the entire group. When in Rome speak as the Romans do! Or try to do so, to the best of your ability.

Leaving hats on while national anthem is being played at sports events. We should be proud to be citizens of our nation. We should display our pride for our country by observing correct protocol. If a father and son are at a game together, please, Dad, stand up straight and remove your hat, and I'm sure your son will automatically do as you do. Be proud of your country and stand respectfully while your national anthem is being played. It is of equal importance to respect the national anthem of any foreign country: this is a simple courtesy and demonstration of respect, the respect that must be accorded to any visitor to your country.

I feel the above tips are the basics we cover every day of our lives. They are not difficult, just plain common sense.

What Is the Purpose of Good Manners?

Good manners are not simply doing what Mom and Dad would do just because that is perceived to be the correct way or blindly following rules. Good manners are about being respectful to others who are younger, older, or your own age and enjoying their respect in return. Good manners are about being considerate to others and being sensitive to your surroundings. For example, thanking a friend if you are loaned a tape or book, thanking Mom or Dad for taking you to the movies or a sporting event. Good manners are not just for special occasions; they are for every moment and, most important, they are for you.

In other words, good manners give you confidence with a capital *C*.

One of the students attending one of my seminars stood up and said, "I don't eat at the Hotel Vancouver on a regular basis. What has all this etiquette got to do with me?"

I replied, "I know. I don't eat at the Hotel Vancouver all the time either, but chewing a hamburger with your mouth wide open at a fast-food restaurant looks just as bad as chewing a slice of steak with your mouth wide open in a restaurant at the Hotel Vancouver! Do not forget, it's the same set of table manners, just different surroundings. I can just imagine what you are thinking! *When will I need this social etiquette?* When you are in school having lunch in the cafeteria, having dinner at a friend's home, attending a party at your friend's or at your own home. Every day opportunities for using social etiquette present themselves, in social circumstances, at school or at work and in your own home. In fact, in every aspect of your everyday lives!"

Children who have had the advantage of being instructed in correct manners as part of their upbringing have a decided advantage over children who have not had this opportunity. Polite behaviour will become second nature to the young person who has had manners and etiquette incorporated in his/her upbringing. These fortunate children are then free to enjoy themselves without fear of embarrassing themselves in any social situation or in the conduct of their lives.

A GOOD PARENT OWES IT TO THEIR CHILDREN TO TEACH MANNERS AS AN INTERESTING AND USEFUL SKILL.

This means that during the period between birth and when children leave home the household should function as follows:

- Families should be conditioned to using appropriate greetings, as a means of expressing courtesy and respect to family and all others.
- Families must master appropriate table manners and be properly instructed in the correct patterns and methods of consuming foods.
- Families must learn civilized alternatives to anger so as to allow their emotion to be expressed without sacrificing family harmony.
- Families must learn to respect the feelings, individualities, and comforts of all others, particularly the fact that guests, regardless of age, ethnicity, or any other difference, deserve to be treated hospitably. As our modern society is now multicultural, particular attention should be devoted to developing conduct that will not be offensive to those of different social origins than the host family.

Once parents learn to observe correct manners and etiquette, they will find it pleasant and rewarding. For children, standards should be carefully outlined but never be unrealistically rigid—and, above all, never cruel. Children as always will continue to make social faux pas, but a knowledgeable parent should be aware of incorrect behaviour and be prepared to patiently and gently correct the children's mistakes.

Etiquette and Manners Are Simply a Means of Expressing Socially Acceptable Behaviour.

Socially acceptable behaviour translates into how you treat others when you care about them, respecting their self-esteem and feelings. Manners are under your control because they come from your heart. In our chaotic world they can make order out of disorder and give you the power to bring pleasure into other people's lives.

Manners relate to the how, what, where, when, and why of the social graces. Learning about manners makes you feel secure in your movements. Manners prevent you from feeling awkward or doing something offensive to others. REAL MANNERS are instructive; they stem from your character and your heart. You don't turn them on and off like a light. They are genuine, because you care about the dignity, welfare, and feelings of others. Correct etiquette is a courtesy to others and a demonstration of your personal consideration. Etiquette should be practiced in all social situations, be it in the home, at the symphony, or at the soccer game.

IT MAKES NO DIFFERENCE HOW YOU LABEL THAT QUALITY OF MOVING ABOUT THE WORLD WITH EASE AND STYLE. GOOD MANNERS OR ETIQUETTE IS HOW YOU TELL THE WORLD THAT YOU HAVE OPTED FOR A SUCCESSFUL LIFESTYLE, AND THE POSITIVE RESULTS IT CAN BRING.

The manners of today are not very different from the manners that were taught many years ago. I just think the approach and the style are different. Trust me, basic manners and etiquette, respect, and confidence building are no different now from those a hundred years ago. The only difference is that good manners are dreadfully lacking in our everyday culture—THIS IS WHAT I WANT TO CHANGE.

2

Table Manners

In 1992, there was a survey taken across Canada that focussed on the ten worst manners that people demonstrated while sitting eating a meal at home or in a restaurant. This is one of the very first things that I address in my seminar.

The survey came up with some good answers. Below is the list developed from the survey, working backwards.

10. Singing
 9. Not joining in conversation
 8. Not passing food
 7. Starting to eat before everyone is seated
 6. Licking fingers
 5. Eating food with knife and licking knife
 4. Shovelling food in as fast as one can
 3. Arguing at the table
 2. Making noises while eating; slurping, etc.
 1. Talking with mouth full

To me number 1 isn't at all surprising. Talking while one has food in his mouth is a disgusting habit. My students listed a lot of these items also, but not necessarily in the same order.

Parents should teach their children table manners. It is parents who initially set the example. Children will copy or mimic parents, so it is their responsibility to help, guide, and remind their offspring of the right way to eat a meal. As the saying goes, "Practice makes perfect."

It is extremely important that parents spend sufficient time at the table with each child, right up through the teen years. This is to make sure that the young person has the opportunity to observe the rudiments of all good table behaviour. Most parents work a long hard day. It has become too easy for each member of the family to "zap" a food choice in the microwave or pick up pizza or "Chinese" to eat in front of the TV. Many families seem to spend more time in front of the TV screen with fast foods in lieu of the family sitting around a table eating with cutlery and discussing what kind of a day they had. Sitting down to dinner with the family is not only a reinforcement of good etiquette, but also is one of the few opportunities for family interaction and communication.

In the nineties everything we have in our homes helps to make our lives run easier and smoother. Part of this "modernity" should include instructing our children in the following long-approved conventions. Our children should know how to sit at the table, the art of joining in conversation, correct use of cutlery, and how to eat their way through a meal nicely.

Parents don't realize how basic table manners can help their offspring in their careers and social situations.

By the time teenagers graduate from high school, they should be at ease at the table.

Do's and Don'ts at the Table

I prefer to be positive when I teach at my seminars, but there are a number of points that are better expressed by the negative. Here are some of the most important "don'ts and do's":

1. Don't talk with your mouth full.
2. Don't chew with your mouth open.
3. Don't lick your fingers or your knife.
4. Don't cut up all your food on your plate; slice off only one piece at a time.
5. Don't return a utensil to the table after it has been used; it must remain on your plate.
6. Don't use your fingers to push food onto your fork. Use your knife.
7. Don't start eating before everyone is served, unless you are told to do so by your host or hostess.
8. Don't encircle a plate with the left arm while eating with the right hand.
9. Don't lean back and announce, "I'm finished," or "I'm full." The fact that you have set your cutlery together on the plate shows that you have finished.
10. Don't put liquid into your mouth if it is already filled with food.
11. Don't wipe off the cutlery in a restaurant; call a waiter.
12. Don't leave your spoon in your cup; it looks unattractive and is dangerous as well.
13. Don't crook your finger when picking up your cup. It is an affected mannerism.
14. Don't put your elbows on the table while you are eating; always keep them close to your sides.
15. Don't make noises while eating—slurping, etc.
16. Don't argue at the table.

1. Do encourage good posture at the table.
2. Do try to have "quiet hands" while at the ta-

ble—leave your hands under the table in your lap or rest them on the table.

3. Do make an effort to join in the conversation at the table.
4. Do pass food before you take it yourself.
5. Do show respect to your dinner companions—USE YOUR MANNERS.

From the moment you approach the dinner table until the moment you push back your chair at the end of the meal, it is important to keep in mind some basic table manners. This has to do with being RESPECTFUL and appreciative towards others and showing that you know how to conduct yourself in a well-informed manner.

Food is served from the left and taken away from the right. Never load your plate—seconds are acceptable and a compliment to the host/hostess. Good dinner-table conversation involves everyone at the table, and by all means avoid subjects that could ruin one's appetite, offend someone, or depress everyone.

Contrary to popular opinion, there is no reason to leave some food on your plate. This practice was born of the belief that finishing everything indicates you really have not had enough to eat. I think this is nonsense. If you are hungry, eat whatever is on your plate. When you have finished your meal, the fork and knife should be placed in the middle of the plate with the handles pointing to 6:30.

It is important to hold your knife and fork correctly. Nothing looks worse than holding a utensil as if it were a dagger. To cut food properly, hold your knife in the right hand and your fork in the left. Pierce the part of the meat closest to you with the fork to keep it steady, and slice off a small piece with your knife. Be sure to use your index fingers to keep both the knife and the fork firm. When you are through cutting, if you eat NORTH AMERICAN style place your knife down on the plate, switch your fork into the other hand, and bring it up to your mouth. If you eat EUROPEAN style, then do not place your knife down after cutting your food and do not switch your fork to the index finger position and then bring it up to your mouth.

I refer to the EUROPEAN or NORTH AMERICAN style of doing things. They are both correct styles of etiquette. I personally use the EUROPEAN style, as I was brought up in England.

The American custom of "zigzag" eating (changing the fork from the left to the right hand after cutting meat), though correct, is, I feel, unnecessarily complicated. Therefore, it does not have as pleasing an appearance as the simpler European method of leaving the fork in your left hand after you have cut your meat. You eat the meat from your fork while it is still in the left hand, rather than turning the fork over and switching it to your right hand.

When it comes to a great meal, delicious food truly can be appreciated only if the setting is attractive and if everyone feels comfortable and confident at the table. There is nothing like an attractive table to make your guests feel welcome. Some people believe that as long as everything is clean and neat, it doesn't matter where you place your dishes or utensils. I am not one of them. I think it is important to lay your table out the correct way. This is so for two reasons:

1. The proper way makes sense.
2. There is something to be said for elegance and tradition. Sticking to "rules" does not mean you are old-fashioned, but rather that you care.

3

Setting the Table

A well-set table might have as few as three pieces of silver at a setting or as many as six or more. It all depends on the occasion, the food, and the time of day. The simpler the setting, the more informal the meal. No matter how you choose to serve, the rules remain the same. Placement is according to use. Each person begins with the outside utensils and works his way in.

If you are serving a quick meal, it is perfectly correct to simply set a fork, knife, and dessert spoon. I occasionally refer to the placement and use of silverware on a plate in terms of telling time on a clock. The handles of the utensils are the arms, and the plate is the face. This makes things very clear.

Flowers, centerpieces, candles, and table napkins really help to make a table look attractive. The only rule that governs the placement of dinner napkins on the table is: keep them attractive. They can sit to the left of the dinner plates with the forks resting either on top or alongside, blossom out of water glasses as if they were flowers, or rest folded neatly flat in the center of the dinner plates or shaped in any number of attractive ways.

As soon as you sit down at the table, spread your napkins across your lap. A luncheon-size napkin should be unfolded the entire way, while a large dinner napkin should be unfolded only in half, before placing it on your lap.

The most important thing to remember about a napkin

"Hands on": setting a table for a formal meal.

Above is a place setting for a formal dinner. Notice the order in which everything is placed. When sitting down to eat, remember to work from the outside in. This place setting is for a five-course meal—soup, fish, salad, entree, or main course, and dessert.

The first piece of cutlery that would be used is the soup spoon (4) on the outside right of the place setting. Working in, the fish fork and knife (1 & 5) are the next two pieces. The third course would be salad (2 & 6). I always serve this as a separate course, but many people serve the salad with the main course. I always set a salad knife as well as a fork; NORTH AMERICAN etiquette usually uses a fork only. The entree knife and fork (3 & 7) lie directly beside the dinner plate. The blades of any knives used must always face inward. Dessertspoon and fork (8 & 9) are placed above the dinner plate, EUROPEAN style: the spoon is used in place of a knife. A butter knife (10) is usually included in the setting, resting across the bread and butter plate (11). In a formal dinner, it is usual to have an entree plate included in the place setting (12). The soup plate, fish plate, and salad plate should always be served on this plate; after the salad course is finished the entree plate should be removed and a fresh entree plate served for the main course.

Water glasses should be placed above the entree knife (7) and wine glasses set out at an angle after the water glasses.

Coffee cups or teacups and saucers are brought out with dessert and placed to the right of the dessert dish. The coffee spoon or teaspoon can be place on the rim of the saucer. Before dessert is served, all serving dishes and condiments from dinner should be cleared from the table.

is that it should stay on your lap until you have risen to leave the table. If you must leave the table during the course of the meal, place your napkin on the seat of your chair, not on the table. It is not very pleasant to see a soiled napkin on the table during the meal. When the meal is over, you may then place your napkin on the table as you get up to leave.

One of the hands-on lessons I have at my seminars includes asking the students to set a formal dinner table. This probably is the only time they will see so much cutlery until they are a lot older. Even the teens are instructed to go through these steps. I also go through the procedure at the adult seminars.

Setting a table for a five-course dinner can be very confusing, but a step-by-step, course-by-course approach helps considerably.

Let us start with our menu:

1. Soup
2. Fish
3. Salad
4. Entree, or main course
5. Dessert

SOUPS: Soup bowls come in two shapes: consommé, which usually has a delicate handle on either side, or a shallow bowl with a rim. Generally, as the names indicate, light cream soups, thin broths, or consommés are served in the former, while thick, chunkier soups are served in the latter. Both soup bowls should be accompanied with a plate beneath them. The spoon, when not in use and when the soup is finished, is laid on the plate. When you are eating the soup, the level of the soup eventually will become so low you must tip the plate to avoid scraping the bottom noisily. Lift the near edge in your left hand and tip the plate away from you. Then the soup may be spooned away from you, which helps to avoid spilling the soup over you.

FISH: There are special fish knives and forks that can be used for a fish course. Usually a fish course is only served at a very formal dinner. The fish knife is pointed at the end to help remove any bones or skin that may be attached to the fish. Usually, fish is served boneless and the skin removed. The fish knife and fork are used in the same way as the entree knife and fork, NORTH AMERICAN or EUROPEAN style.

SALAD: Salad is sometimes served before the entree, or main course, with the entree, or after the entree. I prefer to serve it before the entree and with a salad knife and fork, which are smaller than the main course knife and fork. Again, NORTH AMERICAN style is to serve a fork only with the salad, but EUROPEAN style is to use a knife and fork.

ENTREE, OR MAIN COURSE: A regular-size knife and fork are used, either NORTH AMERICAN style or EUROPEAN STYLE.

DESSERT: This may be eaten with spoon or fork or both. You may use them together *EUROPEAN* style to eat cakes or pastries. The spoon is used in place of a knife. The table should be cleared completely before dessert is served; nothing should be left but the centerpiece, candles, and dessert spoons and forks. Coffee cups or teacups and saucers are set out with dessert and are placed to the right of the dessert dish. You can place your coffee spoon or teaspoon on the rim of the saucer. Coffee, liqueurs, or brandy may be served at the table or taken to another room, whatever the host and hostess decides.

Breads and rolls should always be broken into moderate-size pieces with the fingers before being eaten—but not

"Are we really going to use all this cutlery for one meal?"

"The soup spoon is the first piece of cutlery we use, Mrs. Kennedy."

necessarily single-mouthful bites. To butter your slice or roll, hold a piece on the edge of the bread-and-butter plate and with a butter knife spread enough butter on it for a mouthful or two at a time. There are always commonsense exceptions to the above. For instance, hot biscuits and toast may be buttered all over immediately. However, bread should never be held flat on the palm and buttered with the hand held in the air.

Concerning gravy and sauce; you may sop bread into gravy, but it must be done properly. Put a small piece of bread down on the gravy and eat it with your fork as though it were any other helping on your plate. You may put it into your mouth *EUROPEAN* fashion, with the tines pointed down as they were when you sopped up the gravy. A good sauce may also be finished in this way—in fact, to do so is a compliment to the cook.

With an informal family meal at home, where the atmosphere is more relaxed, do encourage the children, or whoever sets the table, to set it properly, whether it is the kitchen table or the dining room table. The same high standards should apply be it a three- or five-course dinner. If the table is set for each member of the family, it becomes the normal and proper thing to do. This involves all sitting down at the table and going through the process of using a napkin, whether it be paper or cloth, and making correct usage of the cutlery and china that are set out for that particular meal. One of the realities of the 1990s is that both parents work and children are participating in a variety of sports and other activities that occur after school hours. For these reasons, it is sometimes difficult for the entire family to eat together. Parents who do try to have certain meals together as a family should not get into the habit of everyone eating alone or in front of the TV or anywhere else but the table. There is nothing better than a family sitting down to a nice meal discussing what kind of a day they had, be it a positive day or a horrendous day. A sit-down dinner is a good way to keep communication open within the family, and it is truly amazing what can be discussed around the dinner table. Again, this provides children with the confidence to be able to make conversation while at the table, thus reinforcing the social graces we are attempting to teach them.

4

Finger Foods

Some foods require special ways to eat them properly. Some foods can be eaten with the fingers; at certain times they should be eaten with appropriate cutlery. The students at my seminars are asked to list all the foods they can think of that can be eaten with their fingers. I always give them a few hints: for example, when they are at a picnic or barbecue, the movies, a sports event, or a birthday party. It is amazing the information I get, sometimes as many as thirty or forty different food items.

I have listed below some of the most popular finger foods, but remember: when in doubt (especially if you are in someone else's home), use your knife and fork unless your host or hostess invites you to do otherwise. It always looks so much better, and no one will get upset. If you are in a fast-food restaurant most foods are treated as finger foods. At a picnic or barbecue the same applies; I always think it is pure common sense and your surroundings that dictate the way you handle your food.

bread sticks	egg rolls (small)	nachos and
candies	french fries	cheese
cheese wedges	fried chicken	pizza
chips	grapes	raw vegetables
chocolates	hamburgers	sandwiches
cookies	hot dogs	toast
corn on the cob	ice-cream cones	

As well as finger foods, there are other foods that require mentioning, because they may need cutlery different from a knife and fork or require a completely different eating technique.

Artichokes. This vegetable is eaten with the fingers almost completely. Pull off one leaf at a time and dip it into the sauce that is served. Then, holding onto the top of each leaf with your finger, pull the leaf through your teeth to scrape off the soft part at the other end. When all the outer leaves have been scraped and arranged neatly around the side of your plate, remove the fuzzy, prickly part in the middle by cutting under it and lifting it off. Make sure you do not miss any prickes! Then slice the artichoke heart into pieces (one piece at a time), dipping each piece in the sauce with your fork.

Asparagus. Always eat this with your knife and fork.

Chili. Eat with a spoon.

Clams on the half shell. Use your seafood fork to pry the clam out of the half shell. If you want to add horseradish or sauce, spread a little sauce onto the clam in the shell and lift the clam with your seafood fork. Use the same technique for oysters.

Clams, Steamed. Using your fingers, lift out each clam by its neck, then pull the main part of the clam loose and discard the dark neck part. Dip the succulent remains (if you choose) in melted butter and eat in one bite.

Corn on the cob. Place corn on your dinner plate and use a butter knife to spread butter all over. If cob holders have not been provided, lift the corn to your mouth with both hands and nibble away in horizontal lines. Remember, corn on the cob is a North American favorite, as is watermelon. Corn on the cob is usually served at informal dinners, but there can be no excuse for eating it in a manner that may offend others.

French fries. Eat according to where you are: In a fast-food restaurant, french fries are often eaten with the fingers. If you are in a restaurant or dining at a friend's home, knife and fork should be used. You should eat this popular food accordingly—USE COMMON SENSE.

Fried chicken. Again, this is one of the foods people assume is a finger food, but this is not necessarily true. The deciding factor is where it is served. On a picnic certainly use your fingers, but otherwise, steady the piece of chicken on your plate with a fork in one hand and then with your other cut away the meat with a knife.

Hot gravy sandwiches. These should be eaten with a knife and fork.

Lobster. This is correctly served with a tool that looks like a nutcracker. You use it to crack the two big claws first; then you break them apart further with both hands. Next, pick up one of the claws and, with a seafood fork, dig out the meat, and arrange it on your plate. Cut it into bite-size pieces. Finally, dip the lobster morsel in melted butter and enjoy your rich reward for all that hard work.

To get meat out of the small claws, break them with your fingers and either suck out the meat or extricate it with your fork. The coral-colored or green roe of the female lobster are eaten with a fork. This is a delicacy, so don't ignore it! To eat the tail, simply cut down the middle of the underside with a knife and fork. Pull the meat out before you cut it up. If you want, put on that bib! Nobody can eat a lobster neatly, though everyone should try.

Peas. Despite the fact that you might be tempted to pick up these small objects with a spoon, you should always use a fork. If there are a few stubborn peas that refuse to be caught, use your knife to nudge them gently onto your fork. This works equally well for rice!

Pizza. This is usually served sliced into pieces. I usually start eating my pizza with a knife and fork because it is so hot, but as it cools down, it can be picked up and eaten with the fingers, if it is not too messy. Eating pizza with the fingers is accepted as correct behavior.

Rock Cornish game hens. First, cut the hen down the middle; work on removing the meat from the breast by steadying the hen with your fork and using your knife to peel away the meat from the bones. The legs can be a bit more slippery. Use a knife and fork for leg meat.

Shrimp. If the shrimp is small, you can simply spear it with your fork and pop the entire delicacy into your mouth. If it is jumbo size, you can eat it in two bites from the fork! If the shrimp still has the tail part of its shell, you may pick it up with your fingers, or use your knife and fork.

Snails. These delicacies are served in their shells. They are usually cooked with a buttery garlic sauce. First, pick up and hold the shell with the special metal clamps provided. (Snails are usually served very hot.) With your other hand (the one you write with), pull out the snail with a seafood fork and eat it in one bite. Using your fork, dip small pieces of bread inside the shell to absorb (and for you to enjoy) the tasty liquid that remains. Most restaurants now use special escargot dishes to serve snails; this enables the diner to remove the main portion more easily.

Spaghetti. Long spaghetti should be twirled around your fork, not cut up with your knife. Start by twirling a small amount of spaghetti either on a fork alone or, as some people prefer, on a fork held with the tines against the inside of a spoon. Then keep twirling; when the last strand is completely wound put the entire morsel into your mouth.

Stews. These should be eaten with a fork. Liquid can be

soaked up with pieces of bread. Break the bread into the bowl and use your fork to swirl the pieces around.

Etiquette tip. When eating hamburgers, it is much neater to cut these in half. This looks much better than trying to take a huge bite into a whole one, particularly a Big Mac or a Whopper!

I am sure there are many foods I haven't mentioned in this chapter on finger foods, but when you are out dining, eating at a friend's home or in a restaurant, just think what you feel would constitute "good manners," no matter how informal the meal may be.

If in doubt, watch what the majority of other guests are doing and select the demonstrated etiquette that you feel is most correct for the situation. In other words, USE YOUR COMMON SENSE.

5

Telephone Etiquette

Children start taking an interest in the telephone from a very early age, and this is the time to teach them how to use a telephone properly. The telephone should be a pleasant way to communicate, but not everyone feels that it is an easy task to talk on the phone. There are issues the phone introduces that are not present in face-to-face conversations. However, good telephone skills can be mastered.

What parent wouldn't be proud of her young child who answers the phone saying, "Hello, this is Jessica. How may I help you?" or, "If you will hold on, I will get my mom for you." It is quite common, unfortunately, for a child to yell, "Mom, some lady on the phone for you!" If this happens, the child needs to learn some basic telephone etiquette.

A youngster's phone manner can be beneficial to both parents and children. Youngsters can make a good impression on their friends as well as their parents' friends. Mastering different telephone skills—such as taking an important message for Mom or Dad, calling a friend about school, etc.—can help boost a child's self-confidence and increase the confidence of the child in handling situations that require tact and diplomacy.

How do we impress on a youngster the importance of using the phone correctly? In our seminars we have a "hands-on" session with the children—this is not only fun but role-playing that equips the child to deal with actual telephone situations.

The younger the child is when he learns how to use the telephone, the easier it is to teach the child proper telephone etiquette. Help your children feel at ease on the phone by letting them practise early. Buy them a toy telephone to start with and "role-play" with them. It is amazing how many skills they pick up if you create a possible "scenario" via play. Then let them talk to Grandma or Grandpa or favourite aunts or uncles on the phone. If the child doesn't want to talk at first, don't force the issue; wait until he shows some interest. While Grandma may enjoy the child's conversation, others might find it frustrating to have their call answered by a three-year-old. I feel it is better not to subject callers to this when the child is too young to handle calls properly or take messages.

When the child is old enough and has learned his numbers, let him practise dialing when Mom or Dad needs to make a call. In the beginning parents should keep a close watch on which buttons the child pushes—and reinforce the purpose of the telephone as an adjunct to home safety and security.

At this point, parents should make sure children know their home telephone number (and their home address). This is important in case they ever have to call home in an emergency.

By age five or six, most children should be ready to answer the family telephone. Have them answer the phone according to the house rules: "Hello"; "Hello, this is Jessica"; or "Hello, this is the Jones residence."

It is very important to teach a child how to respond when Mom or Dad is not around. Should a child be home alone and receive a call, he should not let the caller know that no adults are present. Instead of saying, "My parents are not here," the child can reply, "My mother cannot come to the phone right now; may I take a message and she will return your call?" The youngster should be instructed to hang up if the caller becomes insistent or questions the child about when the parent will be available.

I would like to mention some of the points I bring up at my seminars.

Incoming Calls.

My students are instructed as follows:

1. Answer the phone pleasantly and clearly.
2. If the call isn't for you and the caller asks for another member of the family, don't call his name out loud. Instead, say, "Just one moment please, I will see if he is available," or, "Hold on please; I will tell my brother you are on the phone." PUT THE PHONE DOWN AND GO AND TELL THE MEMBER OF YOUR FAMILY HE IS WANTED ON THE TELEPHONE.
3. Put the phone down QUIETLY before you go to give the message to any member of your family.
4. If the family member asked for is not at home, take a careful message.
5. If you are not sure of the spelling of the caller's name, ASK.
6. Always repeat the phone number that is given to you.
7. Always ask the caller if there is any message.
8. Speak clearly, so the caller knows you have heard him correctly.
9. If the call is for you, but it is a bad time to speak, say so. Don't rush off the phone saying, "I can't talk

"I'm sorry, my mom isn't available right now. May I take a message?"

"Will you hold the line, please. I will ask my dad to come to the phone."

now"; explain why you would like the person to call back.

Outgoing Calls

1. When you make a call, take the time to speak politely to whoever answers.
2. If your friend's parent picks up the phone, introduce yourself, then ask for your friend: "Hello, Mrs. Jones, this is Jessica speaking. May I please speak with Andrea?"
3. Remember to say "thank you" when your friend's parent tells you to hold the line.
4. If you accidentally dial the wrong number, never say, "Who is this?" It is none of your business! It is your error! Apologize and hang up.
5. When you want to get off the phone, use as much grace and diplomacy as you would if you were talking in person and saying good-bye.

It is an art to be a good conversationalist. It is an art to answer the phone in a pleasing manner that people enjoy. There are some basic communication skills that will go a long way toward helping you express yourself clearly and positively. It is an extremely sensitive and respectful skill to say what you mean and listen carefully to others, leaving them feeling understood and appreciated. It is an art to be a good listener. I do hope adults can learn from this chapter also.

In these days of modern technology there are a number of new gadgets within our telephone systems. One in particular that I dislike is called call waiting. I get very irritated when in the middle of a telephone conversation the person with whom I am talking puts me on hold to answer another call. It is very frustrating and very bad manners. I personally do not like being put "on hold."

Etiquette tip: The person who makes the telephone call is the person who usually ends the call.

6

Common Courtesies

It would make life so much easier if everyone practised basic respect for each other. After all, that is what manners and etiquette are all about. There are so many areas we can cover; here I have covered only a few that are near and dear to my heart.

1. On the street—jaywalking and crossing against traffic lights are illegal and also very dangerous. Drivers are made to slam on brakes, tempers flare, and drivers may become even more aggressive.
2. On the other hand, drivers should be patient and use basic GOOD MANNERS on the road. Except in cases of emergency, forget you have a horn. A blast of your horn just because you are irritated at someone is very bad manners.
3. When driving at night, don't use high beams when cars are coming at you from the other direction.
4. If you are a slow driver, stay in the right-hand lane. Otherwise you can cause havoc with drivers who want to go faster and must therefore do a lot of lane switching.
5. Allow access to people in the ongoing lane when there has been an accident or traffic jam. If everyone takes turns to filter into a lane it is so much easier, and this is good manners.
6. Be patient when you come to a crosswalk and an

elderly or handicapped person is crossing the road. They may be slow, but they cannot help it.

7. Have consideration for other people when you park your car. A sloppy car parker makes life difficult for everyone. When you park, make sure you only take one spot, and don't park too close to other cars, and don't park in the spots reserved for the handicapped.

8. When you are boarding a bus, greet the driver, and say "thank you" when you leave. The driver certainly deserves recognition.

9. Give up your seat to the elderly, handicapped, pregnant women, and women holding babies in their arms; this applies to males or females giving up their seats, especially young children. This used to be the correct thing to do. What a pity that it is no longer common practice.

10. When you go to the movies or theatre you should arrive on time, so that you don't disrupt the performance for other people.

11. Don't rattle candy wrappers or whisper during a performance.

12. When you enter a filled row to take your seat, proceed facing the people in your row, not the stage. In this way the people you are disturbing can look at your face as you apologize.

13. When you are shopping, consider others as you are pushing your cart. Park your cart so that other shoppers can pass you easily with their carts as you stand looking at the goods on the shelf.

14. If you knock something off a shelf or see a packet on the floor of the store, pick it up and put it back on the shelf; it makes pushing a cart so much easier.

15. When you are in the checkout line with a cart full of

groceries and the person behind you only has two or three items, wave him ahead of you.

16. When you are finished unloading the groceries into your car, bring your shopping cart from the parking area to the storage area. If you leave it in the parking area it may make it difficult for other people to park.

17. When you are shopping in a department store, approach the sales clerk pleasantly. A nice smile and a cheery greeting or hello go a long way.

18. Make conversation with whoever is serving you whenever you are waiting for your purchase to be wrapped, etc.

19. Thank the sales clerk for his/her service, however small, and don't forget that smile.

20. If a sales clerk is particularly nice, let his/her superior know. People complain about miserable sales clerks; why not boost the good ones!

21. When you are in a restaurant, treat the waiter with as much respect as you expect to receive.

22. Ask the waiter for his/her name when he/she first approaches your table; never snap your fingers to get his/her attention.

23. Give the waiter your attention when he/she tells you about the specials on the menu and takes your order. They cannot do their job properly if you are not paying attention.

24. If you keep changing your mind, don't lose your temper if your meal isn't as you ordered it.

25. When something does go wrong with your order, do not voice criticisms at the waiter that everyone can hear.

26. When you have good service, tell the waiter/waitress so and tell the manager or owner.

I sincerely believe if the majority of people during the course of their day practised *some* of the common courtesies that I have mentioned above, we would see a significant change towards each other in our society today.

7

Etiquette in the Workplace

This chapter is included in my seminars for young adults and when I go into the workplace. I think it is of utmost importance for young people to know how to behave when they go on interviews or start a new job.

There are different aspects of etiquette in the workplace that I would like to cover, so I will cover these topics separately.

Job interviews. These can be very stressful even under the best circumstances, but if you have a good résumé and go into the interview looking confident and acting like you know what you are talking about, this is a good start. A résumé should include:

Name, address, phone number
Schools attended, grades completed
Degrees or certificates
Courses relating to job being applied for
Interests or hobbies if at all pertinent
Past working experience
Names and addresses of at least three people who would
    be willing to give a reference—previous employers,
    teachers, family doctor, and friends are all good people
    to include

Once an interview is arranged, usually by telephone or letter, you should arrive promptly, dressed neatly and conservatively and should appear serious about getting the job. After being introduced to the interviewer, remember the interviewer's name, and even if he/she is younger than you address him/her as Mr., Miss, Mrs. or Ms. unless told to do otherwise.

If there aren't any ashtrays around, don't smoke. On second thought, don't smoke even if there are ashtrays.

Know as much as possible about the company and the position you are applying for, but do not hesitate to ask questions. Let the interviewer lead the questioning, and do not talk about topics that are not specific to the immediate position.

Make eye contact and shake hands with the interviewers when you arrive and when you leave. Thank him/her for the opportunity. Even if you don't get the job you applied for, send in a carefully prepared thank-you letter indicating that you will be "definitely interested" in any further opportunities that may arise.

Starting a new job. Whatever your position is to be—whether you are a chief executive officer or in the most junior position in your company—simple common sense, respect, and consideration for others are always appropriate in the workplace. If you respect others, you will win respect in return and become part of the team and an asset to your company.

When you start your new job you will need information related to the way business is conducted in your new employment situation. You will also require information related to the following questions:

- What does everybody else do, and how does my new position fit in with the corporate organization?
- What are the "politics" of this organization that has recently employed me and how can I find out?

How do you find these answers? By asking intelligent questions of people when they have time to talk to you. Timing is everything in the business world. And you must learn to be sensitive as well. Never try to take up someone's time when he is on a deadline, rushed, or overloaded with work. By all means, go through those files and correspondence you are encouraged to become familiar with to acquaint yourself with the ethos of your new work environment. It is also important that you talk to customers and clients. But most important of all, you must LISTEN! What you hear all around you is the very best information you will ever receive.

Be pleasant to everyone you work with; it is good for the general atmosphere and morale of the company if you are genuine and friendly. Two things to remember about the workplace:

1. You cannot choose whom you work with, so you are obliged to do your very best *regardless* of what your associates do.
2. The other people in your workplace could easily be the key to the advancement of your career.

Get to know your co-workers as well as you can. Try to eat lunch with them as often as possible. When you relate to other staff members on a relaxed, personal basis, you will be in a better position to learn more about your organization. Also, you will be in a better position to become privy to information that could advance/enhance your career.

Along with business sense and interpersonal skills, a person needs several other assets to be successful in the workplace. If a person is to be respected, liked, and admired by his co-workers, he will need a kind disposition and a good sense of humour and keen awareness of other people's feelings and sensitivities. Being aware of how people feel and being kind to people are synonymous with being sensitive to their needs. This is also a prerequisite to leadership. People who *really* want to work with you will help you get ahead. We all make mistakes at times. Use humour to modify your mistakes. A good sense of humour can alleviate many embarrassing or difficult situations. If you can laugh at yourself when you make a mistake, people will laugh with you, not at you.

- Do be as nice to people in a junior position in your workplace as you are to the boss.
- Don't "rat" on anyone, unless that person is committing a serious offense.
- Don't criticize a co-worker, especially behind his back.
- Do keep your promises; establish a good reputation and keep it.
- Do not gossip.
- Do give credit where credit is due.
- Do return phone calls or at least have someone else do it for you. It is good business sense to do this, but most important, it is basic GOOD MANNERS.
- Do answer correspondence as quickly as possible.
- Do defend at any level of the workplace a co-worker who has been wronged.
- Do show deference and respect to people who are senior.
- Do show compassion to a co-worker who is experiencing grief or stress.
- Don't waste company time with idle chatter or with personal phone calls or visits from friends at the work-place.

Introduction. You do not need to be an executive in the

Office of Protocol to understand the basics of introductions. Put simply, when you are making introductions, remember to present a younger person to an older person first; also, a person of lower rank or status *TO* the person of higher rank or status. For example, you would introduce a friend to your boss, because your boss certainly has rank in your life (and you want to observe protocol). You would introduce your young son or daughter to everyone they meet, because of their youth.

When you introduce yourself to someone, simply say, "Hello, my name is Jessica Smith." If you are in another city, add your hometown to the self-introduction: "Hello, I'm Jessica Smith from Vancouver."

When you are introducing a peer to a peer, it doesn't matter who is introduced to whom. However, it is important to mention *both* first and last names in the introduction. When you are being introduced, concentrate on the name you hear. Repeat it aloud as you say hello. Sometimes using mnemonics—which associates a name with a similar sound or other words—will help you remember a name.

Telephone manners. Cultivate good telephone etiquette in your workplace. Try to place your own calls. Do not put people on hold for long periods of time. Give priority to *face-to-face* clientele over telephone clientele. Apologize for dialing an incorrect number. When you have called a busy person, be aware of the time element and respect any discourtesy. Always place your phone on "call forward" when you are not at your workplace. This will enable someone else to take a message—and for you to return the call. When you go out for a business luncheon or dinner, unless it is absolutely necessary, *leave that cellular phone at the office.*

General behaviour. I personally do not like being around people who have negative attitudes on a daily basis. It brings down the morale of the entire working staff. Also, a situation like this could seriously detract from the work ethic of a staff already productively employed.

When you arrive at your place of work each morning, start the day with a cheery "Good morning" to everyone you meet on the way to your office, machine, counter, or vehicle. It is amazing how people will respond to your greeting!

Etiquette tip: It is basic GOOD MANNERS to greet everyone you know as *you* come into a building. It is not up to the people who are already there to greet you first.

If you are sitting at your desk or at a machine, wherever your place of work is, you should rise from your work station to greet the caller, especially if he is visiting on business from outside. Under certain circumstances this courtesy will not be appropriate if it impedes work flow or production.

Etiquette tip: Never expect anyone who answers to you to follow a rule you do not obey yourself.

MANNERS AND RESPECT should start very early on in life and continue all the way through to the end. They mark your stages of maturation. Your parents and their parents all went through the same stages. You may not like some of the rituals that surround us, but you must also admit that it is so nice to be the centre of attention. It is a compliment to have people paying tribute to you and wishing you well on appropriate occasions. It is important to be thoughtful and considerate to others going through life.

Relationships with everyone as we go through life are very important. The ultimate success of anything you do depends on how nicely you do it. This will enable you to optimize the opportunities that life may present you.

Manners and Etiquette: An Epilogue

At the end of each seminar, I present each student with a certificate of achievement that states each student "has sucessfully completed a seminar on Social Etiquette." I only have the students for a period of six hours, but at the end of each session I hope with all my heart that some of what they have been taught will stay with them the rest of their lives.

I receive much positive feedback from my students and their parents in the forms of letters and phone calls. When I receive a call or letter, I am always so pleased; I feel, after all, here is another getting back to the basics and they will pass on what they have learnt, and I hope it will spread and manners and etiquette will become an important part of our lives once again.